WISE GUIDES

PERIODS

Charlotte Owen

Illustrated by James Tyrrell

Hodder
Children's
Books

A division of Hodder Headline plc

PET

About the author

Charlotte Owen has worked as publicity officer to the Family Planning Association, as researcher for the *Just Seventeen* advice column and as an agony aunt on *19* magazine. She is currently a freelance consultant for both Brook Advisory Centres and the Health Education Authority. She regularly appears on TV and radio.

Acknowledgements

With grateful thanks to Maggie Jones for her invaluable help and encouragement, and to all those who answered my questions and talked to me about their experiences, including amongst others: Carolyn W Evans, Olivia King, William King, Jennifer Koral, Amy McKelvie, Nahi Patel, Ruby Platts-Mill, Chloe Smith, Becky Webster, Hannah, Polly and Sarah.

To my god-daughters: Esther, Poppy, Opie and Maud

Text © Charlotte Owen 1995
Illustrations © James Tyrrell 1995

First published in 1995 by Hodder Children's Books
Originally published as *Everything you ever wanted to know about periods . . . but didn't like to ask!*

10 9 8 7 6

A Catalogue record for this book is available from the British Library.
ISBN 0 340 63604 1

Printed and bound by Mackays of Chatham

Hodder Children's Books
a division of Hodder Headline plc
338 Euston Road
London NW1 3BH

Recommended by Brook Advisory Centres

This book is endorsed by Brook Advisory Centres and was written with their co-operation. By providing research groups and trialling the contents with girls and youth workers in different parts of the U.K., Brook have helped ensure that this book is accessible, up-to-date and relevant to the needs and concerns of young people today.

Brook Advisory Centres was founded in 1964. There are nineteen branches throughout the UK which offer a confidential contraceptive and counselling service to young people. For more information about Brook or for details of your nearest Centre, contact the National Office at the address at the back of this book.

The quotations in this book are taken from the author's interviews with people of all ages.

Introduction

My mother chose the night before my school sports day to talk to my sister and me about periods and the facts of life. The two of us sat and sniggered to cover our embarrassment. She must have guessed her words were falling on deaf ears - she did a repeat performance exactly a year later! Perhaps we learnt a bit more on that occasion, maybe we even asked a few questions - but the truth is that sometimes talking to a parent about periods can be a little cringe-making and awkward. This sometimes prevents us from asking questions in case we appear silly or feel we should already know all the answers. Even I discovered a few more facts while writing this book - I hope it will answer some of your questions.

Charlotte

P.S. There is a list of useful addresses at the back of the book, and a glossary of difficult words. These are marked with an * in the text.

PART ONE

Periods:
what they are

A period is monthly bleeding from the vagina*, an opening between your legs. This bleeding lasts a few days. Most girls have their first period between the ages of 9 and 16. Once they have started, periods happen to all women every month until the age of about 50 when the menopause* or 'change of life' takes place.

Periods are a natural part of every woman's life. They are a sign for women all over the world that they are fertile and that their body is working properly.

I found out about periods and stuff from my parents and from friends. I know the basics, blood comes out, but I don't know all the intimate details.

What else are they called?

Periods are known by a lot of different names. The official, medical term for this monthly bleeding is menstruation*, which comes from the Latin word menses, meaning month.

In the past, periods were not openly talked about, so people used expressions like 'being indisposed' when they had their period. Nowadays girls may simply say that they're 'on' or 'coming on,' have 'the curse', are 'on the rag,' or 'on the blob'.

When do they start?

Most girls will have their first period between the ages of 9 and 16. The average age for periods to start is about 12 or 13. However, many girls start earlier than this and some much later.

If I found out that my mum started late I'd be happy, because then I would be fairly sure that I'd start late too.

The age at which your mother or grandmother started may give you an idea of when you will start, although girls' periods now tend to start earlier than their mothers' did because of better diet and general health. In 1860 the average age for a girl to start her period was 16 and a half, but in 1973 the average was 12 years and 8 months. Today, the average age is 12.

One in ten girls will have their first period while still at primary school.

My periods started when I was 9. I was still at primary school and we hadn't even done sex education yet. My mum had mentioned them, but I was completely unprepared and it was really embarrassing because the school didn't have any towels and there weren't any bins to dispose of them.

Half of all girls will start their periods between the ages of 12 and 14, seven out of a hundred between the ages of 14 and 15 and one out of a hundred at 16 or later.

All my mates had started, all the girls in my year had started, I felt that every girl in the world had begun their periods except me. I was really frightened that I was never going to start, I even went to the doctor about it. I was so excited when I saw that I had, though it wasn't till I was nearly 16.

There's no point in worrying about when you will start; your periods will start when your body is ready. A useful indicator is that periods usually start about two years after the first sign of breast or nipple development or soon after a healthy white fluid starts appearing in your pants. This is called a discharge* and can vary during the month. It often becomes thicker and whiter just before your period starts. If you are worried about not having started your period, try discussing it with a friend or member of your family – if you are still concerned, a doctor or nurse should be able to put your mind at rest.

What is a normal period like?

A period generally begins and ends with a slight, brownish discharge. In between, the blood becomes redder, and the flow heavier.

How long does a period last?

Periods usually last about four or five days. Sometimes they only last two or three days, sometimes as long as seven or eight.

I read about periods in a book and I thought you just had one splurge of blood and that was it. When I found out they went on for days I was really depressed.

My best friend uses slim tampons and only bleeds for two days. I feel big and ugly because I have to use super tampons and I bleed for seven days.

Periods generally start light and are heavier for just a couple of days. However, the length and heaviness of a period is different in each person, so don't worry if your periods are usually heavy for the whole time or even very light - this is quite normal.

How regular are periods?

Many women have a menstrual cycle* of about 28 days. In other words, their period starts 28 days after the last one started. Some girls and women have shorter cycles, sometimes as short as 21 days, while others have longer cycles, such as 35 days. Some girls find that their periods are not completely regular, but this is nothing to worry about, especially when your periods first start.

For the first year or so your periods may be very irregular. After a while they will probably settle down. Use a diary to mark down the days when you have your period over the next six months and you may begin to see a pattern. You should be able to work out the average length of time between your periods, which will help you know when to expect them. (Use the calendar on page 90 to help you work out the length of your cycle.)

I pretended at school I'd started a year before I had - I even put little crosses in my diary and left it lying around, but nobody noticed, which was lucky really, because when I did start, my periods were really irregular at first.

Do women ever miss periods?

Yes, they do. Sometimes a woman's menstrual cycle seems to miss a month, and the period starts normally again after a month's gap. This is more common when they first start having periods, or later on when a woman is approaching the menopause (this is the time in a woman's life when she stops having periods and is no longer able to have babies).

Women do not have periods while they are pregnant, so missing a period can be the first sign that you are going to have a baby. If you are having sex and you are late with a period, you should always go to a Brook Advisory Centre, a family planning clinic or a doctor for a pregnancy test straight away.

You can also miss periods if you lose a lot of weight, are very stressed (for example before exams) when travelling or during a family crisis, or if you are regularly involved in strenuous physical activity (for example if you are a full-time ballerina or athlete). Amenorrhoea* is the medical term for this missing of periods when you're not pregnant.

How much blood do you lose?

Much less than it looks. Although periods may last up to a week, very little blood is actually lost.

Doctors say that, on average, about four to six tablespoons of blood are lost, although the amount does vary widely among women. If you are worried about the amount of blood you are losing, consult your doctor.

What does it feel like?

The sensation of losing blood through the vagina can feel strange and awkward at first, rather as if you are accidentally peeing. The fact that the menstrual flow can't be controlled in the same way as going to the toilet makes some women feel awkward and ashamed. Because we may have been told off as children for wetting or dirtying ourselves, these feelings of shame sometimes linger on.

> It was a bit like starting a new school. Even though I knew what was happening it was a bit scary. When I first started I thought it was going to be uncomfortable, but actually I felt good, in the same way as when I got my first bra.

In fact, you may not be aware of the sensation at first, but only become aware of the blood as it cools outside your body. If your period is heavy, you may feel a gush of blood which often seems to be more than it really is.

It's a bit like the first time I went to Paris - my parents told me all about it and I looked at pictures in books, but I didn't really know what it was like till I got there.

Do periods hurt?

Many women do have painful periods at some time in their lives, although a lot of women are lucky and never experience bad period pains.

Sometimes you may feel a dull aching in the lower part of your belly, or a kind of cramping pain. These are usually called 'period pains' or by the medical term dysmenorrhoea*.

I get a cramping pain like my insides are being scrunched up, and it's embarrassing. You can't tell anybody because they'll think you're being flaky.

Period pains can be worse if you are worried and tense all your muscles. Some girls do this instinctively to try and 'hold on' to the blood flow because they are worried about staining their clothes. Rather than worrying about this, if you have period pains, the best thing to do is relax, preferably in a warm place. If you're at home, curling up under the duvet with a hot water bottle and relaxing for a while can help. Some schools may have a quiet room you can sit in, or you could take a painkiller to help you relax.

Once I got them in my English class so badly that I wanted to die. I went to the school nurse and she told me to walk up and down the corridor - and it worked, it really did help!

Really painful periods may be a sign that something is wrong, so you should always check with your doctor. If your periods aren't that bad but you're still worried, it can help to talk to an adult (like your mother or a teacher at school) who knows about periods and may be able to reassure you. If your doctor is a man and is part of a practice with more than one doctor, you can always ask the receptionist if you can see a woman doctor or the practice nurse. Although you may think a woman doctor will be more sympathetic, this isn't necessarily so, as male doctors are just as used to chatting with women patients about these problems.

Do you have to take things easy when you have a period?

There's no reason why you shouldn't carry on with all your normal activities when you have a period, and many women find that exercise actually helps relieve period pain by stretching out all the muscles. In fact, when you are being energetic your body releases endorphins, which are the body's natural painkillers.

However, it's also perfectly all right not to take part in vigorous exercise if you don't feel like it. Running around may make your period seem heavier, as the blood will flow out more quickly, so you may not want to. Blood is usually a sign that your body is damaged, so it's not surprising that bleeding from your vagina, even though in this case it's a sign of health, makes you feel instinctively that it must hurt, or that you want to rest and protect yourself. These feelings are perfectly normal.

'Whatever feels right for you...'

You may also feel more tired than usual, and if you do, don't push yourself. Some girls find it helps to take vitamin pills containing iron, but best of all is to eat a healthy diet - nuts, green vegetables and red meat are all good for replacing iron you may lose in period blood.

What about swimming and other sports?

There is no reason why you can't swim if you want to, as the pressure of the water stops the flow of your period while you are in the pool. However, if you are wearing pads or towels, you might prefer not to swim, as you will have to remove your sanitary protection*. But if you do, make sure you have some towels handy for after you get out. If you wear tampons, there is no problem swimming with them in place. In fact, many girls and women say that the exercise makes them feel better.

I'd probably avoid contact sports such as rugby or football, but exercise like skating or running would be fine. I don't think that sports that are over-straining are good for you when you've got your period.

So, it's fine to take part in energetic sports if you want to join in, but if you don't feel up to it, that's fine too.

What about having a bath or washing your hair?

There is no reason at all why you shouldn't do these things. Personal hygiene is important at all times, not just when you have your period.

Sometimes I get a bit of a tummy ache and generally feel a bit washed out, especially on the first day or two of my period. Lazing in a bubble bath with the door shut and listening to one of my favourite tapes on my Walkman while I soak always perks me up - until the rest of the family start banging on the door wanting to use the bathroom!

Not washing your hair is an old wives' tale dating back to a time when women who had periods were considered taboo and had to shut themselves away, not taking part in normal activities. A taboo is something that is forbidden, usually because it is considered holy or unclean.

Are periods still taboo in some cultures?

Many girls growing up in Sikh, Hindu, Islamic and other cultures find that when they reach puberty there are certain rules that they are expected to follow. For instance, a Sikh girl at puberty is expected to change the way she dresses. Many of these guide-lines are to do with cleanliness and hygiene. For example, under the Islamic faith it is suggested that a woman has a complete bath after the end of her cycle; this ritual bath is called *Ghusi*.

When I've got my period my parents don't expect me to go to the Temple for prayers with them. I don't really mind, in fact I think quite the opposite, it's not necessarily a bad thing at all. My brother gets sulky and grumpy as he has to go off with the family and I get a bit of peace and quiet at home. Sometimes I even wish I had my period twice a month!

A lot of religions say that a woman shouldn't go to a temple and pray when she is menstruating. In fact a lot of these taboos aren't actually written down in religious books, but are traditions which have been handed down from generation to generation. In the same way, in some parts of Africa, girls may be banned from picking crops, cooking or other activities when they have their period because it is thought the food will spoil or the crops fail.

Blood is also a sign that a woman isn't pregnant, so a taboo against menstruation can be stronger in societies where women are viewed only as wives and mothers.

Today we are luckier than previous generations, because periods are more openly discussed and better sanitary protection is available enabling us to carry on with life as normal. Our grandmother's generation had a much harder time.

When I was young we never talked about periods and things like that. I started when I was 13 and I hadn't the slightest idea what was happening to me. When I saw blood on my pants I looked everywhere for a cut, and when it kept coming I thought I must have some terrible disease. I was afraid to ask anyone because I thought they would tell me I was going to die. When I did tell my mother, she and my aunt whispered together and gave me some bulky towels to wear, and that was all we ever said about it.

In order to get rid of the idea of a menstrual taboo completely, some mothers in America have started celebrating their daughter's first period with a party to which family and friends are invited. Some American women have 'bleed in' parties where they all get together when they have their period. So far it hasn't happened here!

What can I wear?

Nowadays, with modern sanitary towels and
tampons, you can wear whatever you like, even
body-hugging skirts and leggings. However, on the
days when your period is heavy, you may prefer not
to wear pale-coloured clothes or things that are too
tight, as it will be more obvious if you leak.

I always get my period at the same time as my sister - is that normal?

It's quite common for women who are living in the
same house or spending a lot of time together to have
their periods at the same time. This is because
hormonal signals are passed from one to the other in
sweat, but nobody quite knows how. It's certainly
nothing to worry about.

*I always get my period the same time as two of my best
friends, we always all come on the same week.*

● QUIZ ●

Question:

It's sports day at school, you're a bit of a star in the PE class but you've got your period, do you:

a) Make your excuses and sit by the side of the sports field?

b) Get out there and do your best?

Answer:

a) There's no truth in any of the old wives' tales that say you can't be active during your period. Some girls may simply feel better if they're curled up in a chair rather than rushing around. It's up to you.

b) There's no medical reason why you shouldn't play sports - it depends what you feel like. In fact, being energetic actually helps relieve period pain, by stretching your muscles and releasing the body's natural painkillers, endorphins.

Question:

What is the average age a girl may expect to start her period?

a) between 12 and 14

b) between 17 and 19

Answer:

a) Between 12 and 14 is the average age, although it is quite normal for girls to start both earlier or later than this.

b) Approximately 1% of girls start their periods at the age of 16 or later. Your periods will start when your body is ready, but if you're worried, consult your doctor to put your mind at rest.

Question:

On average, how much blood is lost during a period?
a) 4-6 tablespoons
b) A bowlful

Answer:

b) 4-6 tablespoons is the average amount of blood lost during a period.
c) It may look like you are losing more blood than you think but it isn't very much really. Put 4-6 tablespoons of water in a bowl and see.

PART TWO

Periods:
why we have them

Periods: why we have them

Periods are part of the natural cycle of a woman's body which enables her to have children. When your periods start you may still feel far away from having a sexual relationship or having a baby, but it is a sign that your body is ready.

Once you reach puberty, one of your two ovaries* releases an egg cell, or ovum*, every month. The egg cell can be fertilised if you have sex and sperm enters your vagina. Fertilised or not, the egg cell travels down the Fallopian tube* to the womb.

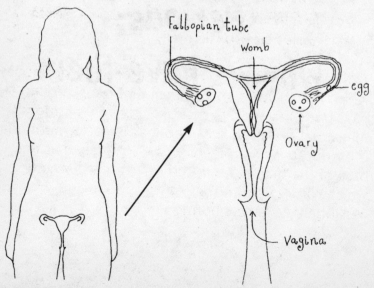

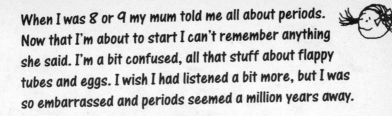

When I was 8 or 9 my mum told me all about periods. Now that I'm about to start I can't remember anything she said. I'm a bit confused, all that stuff about flappy tubes and eggs. I wish I had listened a bit more, but I was so embarrassed and periods seemed a million years away.

If the egg cell is not fertilised by joining up with a sperm, it cannot develop into a baby, so is broken down and reabsorbed by the body. Meanwhile the inside of the womb has developed a thicker lining, rich with blood vessels, as it gets ready for a fertilised egg to implant and grow. But if the egg cell isn't fertilised, this isn't needed either. So the lining of the womb breaks away, causing a small amount of bleeding, and, through contractions of the womb, this blood and the womb lining are expelled from the body. This is what is known as a period.

I wondered where the blood was coming from, if it came from the fatty bits on my arm. Then somebody explained that it came from inside the womb.

This regular monthly cycle is controlled by hormones*, which are chemical messengers that travel around your body in your bloodstream. Before your monthly menstrual cycle can start, though, a master hormone is produced by the pituitary gland*, a gland at the base of the brain. This in turn releases a hormone which causes your ovaries to start producing oestrogen*, a female hormone.

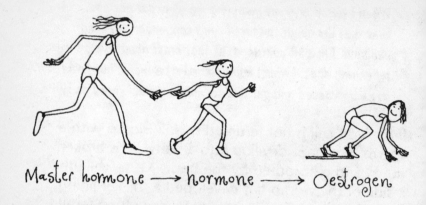

Master hormone ⟶ hormone ⟶ Oestrogen

It is oestrogen which starts off the changes you begin to experience at puberty. Your breasts start to swell, and sometimes the area around the nipple darkens. Girls normally grow taller around this time and may notice that their body outline changes, with the hips becoming wider, creating a womanly curve. Hair also starts to grow between your legs and under your arms.

Once all this happens, your body starts to experience the normal monthly menstrual cycle. The pituitary gland releases a hormone every month which makes some of the hundreds of thousands of immature egg cells in the ovaries start to ripen. The ovaries send another hormone message to the womb, telling its lining to thicken to receive the egg. When the first egg cell is ripe, another hormone makes it burst out of the ovary and travel into the Fallopian tube. This moment of egg release is called ovulation*.

Will I notice the moment I ovulate?

O ccasionally girls and women say they feel a slight pain in the middle of their monthly cycle, between their periods, when the egg cell is released. This pain is sometimes called mittelschmertz, a German word meaning simply 'middle pain'. Many girls and women notice that they have a slight, whitish, yellowish or jelly-like vaginal discharge in the middle of the month. This is called ovulation mucus, and comes from the cervix, the entrance to the womb. It is designed to help sperm swim up from the vagina and into the womb in search of the egg cell. Women can learn to recognise this mucus, which shows when they are most fertile during the month and most likely to conceive a baby.

While this discharge is most obvious in the middle of the month, the vagina always produces some discharge which helps remove any bacteria and keeps the vagina clean. You may notice that this fluid changes slightly during the month. This is quite normal, as long as it does not smell or itch. There is no need to use a vaginal deodorant or wear panty liners. Often this discharge starts before your periods begin and may be a sign that they will start soon.

I started getting whitish stains on my pants. I was really worried and thought that bits of my insides were coming out and maybe there was something really wrong with me. My mum told me that it was healthy and soon my periods would start, I thought she was making it up but she was right, and they did start.

How is the egg cell fertilised?

The egg cell can be fertilised if a girl or woman has unprotected sex with a boy or man during which his penis enters into her vagina and he ejaculates* semen, which is the liquid which contains the sperm. The egg cell can also be fertilised if he ejaculates very near to the vagina, without even putting his penis in, as some sperm may still find their way up inside the vagina. The sperm swim up the vagina, into the womb and up to the Fallopian tubes. Just one lucky sperm will fertilise the egg!

Sex isn't just about having babies, it's also a pleasurable way in which two people can show that they care about one another and are very close to one another. If they don't want to have a child, they can use contraception (e.g. the Pill, I.U.D. (coil), cap, or condom) to protect against pregnancy. (See Part Five for more information about sexual relationships.)

What happens after the egg cell is released?

Once the egg cell is released, the part of the ovary it came from releases a second hormone, progesterone*, which prepares the lining of the womb to receive the egg cell once it is fertilised.

What happens if the egg cell is fertilised?

If the egg cell is fertilised, it moves down from the Fallopian tube into the womb, where it settles into the blood-rich, spongy lining and begins to develop into a baby. Hormones produced by the ovary in response to this fertilisation keep the pregnancy going until the placenta*, which nourishes the baby, is large enough to take over. This happens at about three months.

What if it's not fertilised?

When the egg cell is unfertilised, the levels of both oestrogen and progesterone fall away. This sends a signal to the pituitary gland that there's no pregnancy. The whole cycle then starts again. The lining of the womb breaks up and results in a period.

In fact, you can have a period without having released an egg cell at all. This is quite common in young girls just starting their periods, because the whole cycle is just getting going, like a trial run.

Do these hormones have other effects?

The changing levels of hormones every month can make women moody and unpredictable. In particular, women sometimes feel tense and irritable just before their period - this is known either as pre-menstrual tension* (PMT) or pre-menstrual syndrome* (PMS), and is caused by the falling levels of the hormones oestrogen and progesterone.

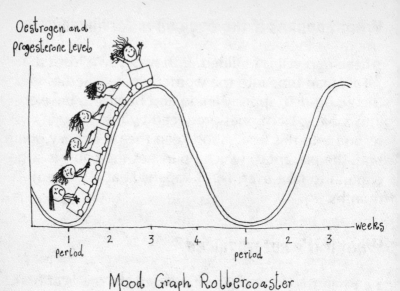

Oestrogen and progesterone level

weeks

1   2   3   4   1   2   3

period   period

Mood Graph Rollercoaster

My moods are changing – sometimes I feel really good after crying for no reason at all.

Not every girl or woman experiences PMT, but many do. It is quite rare for girls who are just starting their periods, but may happen after you have been having your periods for a while. Some girls say they feel tired and that it can be difficult to concentrate. Others say they feel weepy and depressed.

I get all weepy just before my period, crying at anything from programmes about Battersea Dogs' Home to Tottenham Hotspur losing a match.

Still others find that they suffer to different degrees from character changes. Some people always flare up and have a row with their parents, boyfriend or friends just before their period starts, others suffer mood swings and can feel quite violent, even though they are normally quiet, even-tempered individuals.

I sometimes feel like screaming. I just want to lock myself in my room, I feel so horrible and hate everything.

Some girls will notice that their mums or older sisters can get very bad-tempered just before they get their period. It helps if you can understand why they're like this and be considerate to them at this time.

The whole family knows when mum's about to get her period as she gets in a bad mood - I suppose it becomes part of your life, and you just have to accept that you will feel a bit grumpy.

Some people find that taking vitamin B6 or Evening Primrose Oil supplements helps with PMT. Others find that eating a healthy diet of fresh fruit and vegetables, while avoiding fizzy drinks, coffee, sugar and fatty foods helps to alleviate the symptoms of PMT.

Are there any other effects?

Some girls find that their hair and skin seem greasier and they tend to get spots when their period is due. Some find that their breasts feel slightly tender or uncomfortable. Others find that they tend to 'bloat' or swell up slightly as their bodies hold on to water (water retention*) in the few days before their period. It's said that Marilyn Monroe had to have different size dresses while filming to take into account her weight change before and after a period!

Avoiding salty foods can help prevent water retention, but if this is a real problem for you there are pills you can take called diuretics*. However, these can be dangerous, so always talk to a doctor before taking them.

If I don't eat when I've got my period I feel really wobbly and awful. At the beginning of my period I always want to eat sweet things, so I try to eat an apple or a banana instead.

It is common to feel tired, or even dizzy and faint, when your period is just starting or is at its heaviest. One of the reasons for this is because your body's metabolism* is affected by the falling hormone levels, and you may have low blood sugar. The best thing to do is to eat regular healthy snacks such as apples, muesli bars or brown bread throughout the day. This will keep your blood sugar at a steady level.

If anything goes wrong I grab a box of choccies.

Eating very sugary things may make you feel better straight away, but actually only makes things worse, as your blood sugar level will drop suddenly soon afterwards.

Can you tell when your period is due?

Once your menstrual cycle is established, you can usually predict when your period will start by keeping a record of the dates of your period and looking at the calendar. You may be able to recognise the physical symptoms that tell you your period will probably start in a day or two.

I know when I'm going to come on as I get this funny aching on either side at the top of my legs and I normally start a week later.

I get aching breasts and I feel really bad-tempered just the day or two before it starts.

Most women find that their cycle eventually settles down to somewhere between every 25 and 35 days. It can take up to a year or more for periods to settle down, and some women never have a regular cycle. Everyone's body behaves in a different way.

You can't predict exactly when your period will begin each month - it can be at any time. Some women find their period starts quite slowly, others quite suddenly. So it's worth being prepared and carrying towels or tampons around in your bag at the time you think your period is due.

The first few times I got my period I was never expecting it. I remember sitting there in Maths and having this warm sticky feeling between my legs - I thought I'd wet myself, and it wasn't until break when I ran into the loo that I saw there was a bit of blood.

Can you tell when other girls or women have a period?

A quarter of women between the ages of about 10 and 50 will be having their periods at any one time. But if you look around you at school, on the

You just can't tell who's got their period

train or in a crowd, you'll see that there is no way of telling if someone has their period just by looking at them - so don't feel self-conscious!

Can your period stop and start again?

I always use a tampon for the first few days, but the last day or two my period seems to stop and start and it's much harder to put a tampon in – it feels dry, so I just use pads.

It's quite common for your period to seem to stop after the first two or three days when it's heavier, but then start up again, especially if you're physically active. For example, it often won't seem so heavy when you're lying down, and may seem to have stopped altogether when you get up in the morning. Remembering this, and carrying a pad or tampon with you can save you from an embarrassing situation.

● QUIZ ●

Question:

You're at your best friend's house and discover that your period has started. Do you:

a) Feel uncomfortable, hardly dare to sit down in case you leak, and rush off to the bathroom every half hour to make towels out of loo paper?

b) Tell your friend or her mum?

Answer:

a) Periods don't always start at convenient times, as every woman knows. Rather than worrying, remember that this will have happened to everyone at some time.

b) Most women will have a pad or tampon you can use if you get 'caught short'. If it happens at school, tell a female teacher who should be able to find something for you to use.

Question:

You're feeling grumpy. Do you

a) Eat five Mars Bars.

b) Scream at your kid brother.

c) Tell someone how you're feeling.

Answer:

a) Stuffing yourself with chocolate may give you a temporary boost, but won't solve the problem as you'll soon have a low blood sugar level again. It will also leave you feeling unhealthy and, in the long run, wreak havoc with your weight!

b) We can all get a bit down at times, but try not to take it out on your family and friends. You'll probably end up saying things that you don't mean.

c) Talking to somebody sympathetic can make the world of difference. At times it can be comforting to have an understanding shoulder to cry on.

PART THREE

Towels
and tampons

When you have your period, you will need to use sanitary towels or tampons to absorb the blood. In this respect, modern girls are much better off than at any other time.

Modern sanitary towels are extremely light, absorbent and discreet, and don't have all the pads, belts, loops and pins which your mother's generation had to cope with. Most are very small, attractively wrapped and easy to carry around in your bag - and are almost impossible to spot when you are wearing them. Tampons allow you even more freedom.

What are sanitary towels like?

Modern sanitary towels (STs or pads) are made of paper or wood pulp and cotton-like material and are highly absorbent. Most are shaped to fit the area between your legs and have strips which can be pulled off to reveal a backing which sticks to your pants. This is enough to keep the pad firmly in place during all but the most vigorous activities. Pads with side flaps or 'wings' stick to your pants from the sides as well as underneath and may give extra security, for example, if you are jumping and twisting in the gym.

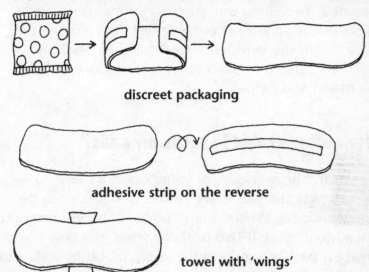

discreet packaging

adhesive strip on the reverse

towel with 'wings'

STs usually come in different thicknesses and degrees of absorbency for the different days of your period, when the flow is lighter or heavier. If your flow is very heavy, you may find that a little blood leaks round the edges, so it can help to wear darker coloured pants which won't show the blood, and perhaps wear an extra pair.

I'll never forget my first date. We went to the cinema and...you've guessed it...my period started. I rushed off to the toilets and rinsed my knickers out and made a poor attempt at drying them under the hand dryer. Then, of course, I didn't have any change for the sanitary towel machine and had to go out again and ask Steve for some. He was great about it, it made us much closer, and yes, we're still going out together now.

However careful you are, there may be times when you find that blood will leak, and your pants will get stained. You'll find that running your clothes under cool water as soon as possible will help remove the blood and prevent permanent staining. Soaking stained pants in a biological washing powder before washing also helps.

How often should I change my pads?

For the heavier days of your period it's best to change the pad every couple of hours or so, to prevent leaks. When your period is light, you may only need to change it two or three times in a day. If you leave a pad on too long the warm blood may start to smell, or the damp towel may chafe your skin and make it sore.

 Some towels say you have to change them 10 times a day. They would, wouldn't they? It's the manufacturers trying to make money.

Buying sanitary protection

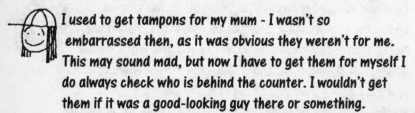 I used to get tampons for my mum - I wasn't so embarrassed then, as it was obvious they weren't for me. This may sound mad, but now I have to get them for myself I do always check who is behind the counter. I wouldn't get them if it was a good-looking guy there or something.

I'd rather buy sanitary towels if a man was serving, as I'd imagine he wouldn't ask me any questions.

Don't be embarrassed about going into a shop and buying towels or tampons. All women do it, and they're for sale in supermarkets, petrol stations, late night shops, newsagents, slot machines in restaurants and cinemas - in fact, just about everywhere.

I worked in a chemist's for my summer job, and I got really fed up with all these people who came in, peered at all the shelves, looked feeble and went out again without buying anything.

I wish someone had told me what sanitary protection to use. I was too embarrassed to ask in the chemist's and there were so many to choose from.

You don't have to go into a chemist's, though you'll find the biggest choice there.

I feel embarrassed about asking which size would be best or anything like that, I just put them on the counter and don't say anything, because I think they must be as embarrassed as I am.

Sometimes girls get their mothers to buy their towels when they first start, but you may find you prefer to choose your own brands and try out which work best for you. You could also ask friends which brands they use, to give you an idea.

I kept changing brands. I'd find a brand I liked, then I couldn't find it again!

How do I dispose of them?

In public lavatories and in some schools and colleges, special bins are provided for you to dispose of towels. If they're available, it is best to use these rather than flushing the towel down the loo. Remember that sanitary towels can block the plumbing, and that it probably won't be you who has to unblock it – so take pity! Only flush towels as a last resort. Instead, wrap them up well in paper and put them in the nearest bin. This is kinder on your plumber and on the environment!

There are some situations, for instance when you're camping or staying in a foreign place where the plumbing is dodgy, where disposal may be a problem.

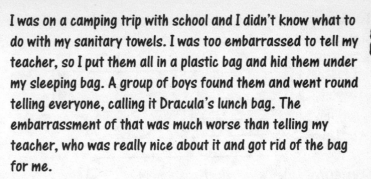

I was on a camping trip with school and I didn't know what to do with my sanitary towels. I was too embarrassed to tell my teacher, so I put them all in a plastic bag and hid them under my sleeping bag. A group of boys found them and went round telling everyone, calling it Dracula's lunch bag. The embarrassment of that was much worse than telling my teacher, who was really nice about it and got rid of the bag for me.

You can wrap your soiled towels in a plastic bag and get rid of them with the rubbish, but they may need to be disposed of quite soon in hot weather so they don't smell unpleasant.

What about tampons?

Tampons are tight rolls of cotton wool with a cord attached to one end. You push the tampon into the vagina with an applicator or your finger and leave it there to absorb the blood flow. When you need to change it, you pull it out by the cord and dispose of it.

It's better for the environment if you can bin your tampons, but, if there isn't a bin in the toilet or washroom you are using, you can usually flush them down the toilet quite easily.

As with pads, tampons come in different sizes and degrees of absorbency, usually light, regular, super, or super plus. You may need different absorbencies for different days, depending on how heavy your period is. Always use the lowest possible absorbency for your flow.

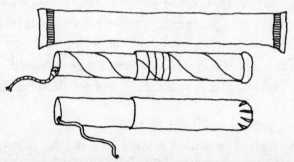

applicator tampons, wrapped and unwrapped

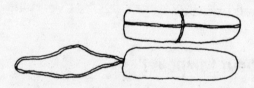

non-applicator tampons, wrapped and unwrapped

You need to change tampons about as often as you change an external pad or towel. You may need to change your tampon every hour or so when the flow is very heavy, but every three or four hours is normally about average. You can tell when a tampon needs changing because you will notice the cord is blood-stained or some blood is leaking out, and you may well notice a trickling sensation when this happens. It can help simply to change it routinely when you go to the loo to avoid this happening.

If the tampon is wet, it will usually slip out very easily. If you give it a tug and it seems to stick, it's usually dry and may not need changing. However, you should never leave a tampon in for hours and hours because of the very remote possibility of it causing an infection. You must always change your tampon when you go to bed at night and when you wake up in the morning, as it's not a good idea to leave it in longer than overnight. When their periods are very heavy, or at night, some girls and women like to wear a towel as an extra precaution to prevent leaking.

Which kind of tampon should I use?

Some tampons come with a cardboard or plastic tube applicator, others are simply pushed in with a clean finger. Try different ones and see which you prefer.

Some women can't manage with an applicator and actually remove the applicator if a friend lends them the 'wrong' kind, so they can push the tampon in with their finger.

I tried the tampons with the cardboard tube and I hated them - they were so big and I thought they would hurt me and I just couldn't manage it. Then I tried the small ones without an applicator and found they went in quite easily.

Others prefer to stick with cardboard or plastic applicators.

My mum uses those tampons without an applicator and gave me them to try, but I just couldn't get them in. Then one day I was round at a friend's house and saw that she had the other sort - the ones with a tube to put them in. I had a go with hers and hey presto! I've never looked back.

Can a tampon fall out?

The tampon is held securely in place by the muscular walls of the vagina, and will not fall out. Occasionally, if you are straining to go to the toilet, you may push out the tampon by accident. This is because the vagina and anus* are next to each other and their muscles often work side by side. If this happens, simply put a new tampon back in.

Can I use a tampon if I am a virgin?

Yes, you can. A virgin is a girl or boy who has never had sex. Plenty of women use tampons even though they have never had sex.

 Someone once told me that you couldn't use a tampon if you were too young or if you were a virgin. I am a virgin and I don't know what too young means or how old you have to be before you can use one.

People used to think that virginity was shown by a physical sign, i.e. an unbroken hymen*. The hymen is a thin layer of skin partly covering the entrance to the vagina. But using the hymen as a sign of virginity is misleading, as it can be broken or stretched in lots of ways other than through having sex. Vigorous exercise, like gymnastics, cycling or horse-riding, is often responsible for the hymen breaking. This often happens without a girl being aware of it, usually some years before she actually 'loses her virginity' through having sex.

> Before I got my period when I was 11, I was worried that I
> wouldn't be able to put a tampon in, so I stole one of my
> sister's and put it in following the instructions. I went around
> with it in all day feeling that I had a big secret. Afterwards I
> thought I wouldn't be a virgin any more but I was afraid to
> ask my sister because I knew she'd be mad at me.

Using tampons makes no difference to your virginity.
You can only 'lose your virginity' by having sex.

If you don't like the idea of inserting anything into
your vagina, it is better to use a towel and wait until
you feel ready to try tampons.

My mother doesn't approve of tampons.

Some women do not approve of young girls using
tampons, even if they're quite happy for women
who are no longer virgins or who have had children
to use them. This may be to do with the way they
were brought up, or because their own mother didn't
allow them to use tampons. If you want to try
tampons and your mother isn't sympathetic, try
discussing it with a school friend who's using them, an
older sister or any woman you trust, or with a school
or practice nurse.

How do I put a tampon in?

First wash your hands, so that you don't transfer any
germs onto the tampon and into your vagina.
It is very important to relax. If you are not certain
about your anatomy, it can help to have a good look

at your genital region with a mirror - a hand-held one is probably best. Open the folds of skin - the labia* or lips - around the entrance to the vagina and have a look. You will be able to see the anus, the clitoris* and the skin round the vaginal opening (see diagram on page 81). You can use your fingers to try to locate the vaginal opening by feeling around.

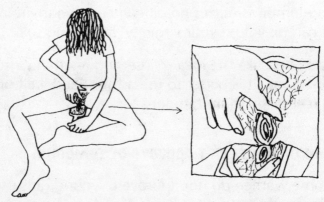

If you insert your first tampon when the flow is heavy, the vaginal walls will be moist and slippery and this will help the tampon to slip in.

 A friend showed me how to use tampons - she put one in in front of me just to show me how easy it was.

If you are using an applicator, make sure the cord is hanging out of the end of the tube before sliding it in gently. Push up the inner tube to press the tampon out, then withdraw the whole tube. If you are using a tampon without an applicator, use your finger to push the tampon in. Remember to pull the cord out first so it hangs outside of the vagina and makes it easy to remove the tampon. The vagina points upwards and backwards towards the small of your back, so push

the tampon in at this angle. Try to relax, as this will
help it go in more easily.

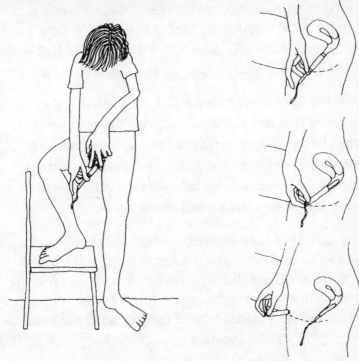

*It wasn't until I read the instructions properly on the packet
of tampons that I realised my vagina pointed backwards,
not straight up! No-one had told me that before.*

Push the tampon in as far as feels comfortable. Only
about the outer third of the vagina is capable of feeling
sensation, so if it isn't in far enough you will feel the
tampon and this will be uncomfortable. You'll know
you've got it in right when you can't feel it's there.
Don't worry about pushing it in too far; you can't.
There is no way that you can push the tampon up into
the womb, or cause yourself any damage.

What if I can't get it in?

Remember that the vagina is capable of stretching quite wide enough to take a man's penis and for a baby to pass through, so it's not going to be too small to take a tampon!

I tried for ages to get a tampon in, I'd lock myself in the bathroom for hours pushing and pulling, I'd even try when I didn't have my period. In the end I gave up for a few months, and then, when I didn't really care, I had another go, and it worked. I'd been so worried before that I'd got completely tense and I'm sure that's why it wouldn't go in.

Many girls find that when they first start their periods they can't cope with using a tampon. If you try and don't succeed, don't worry, give it a rest for a month or two, use a pad and try again later. Never try to insert a tampon unless you're having a period because your vagina will be too dry.

What if I can't get it out?

It is extremely unusual to be unable to remove a tampon. Sometimes the string may get caught up inside the vagina and you may have to use your finger to tease it out or to grip the end of the tampon. Make sure you wash your hands first.

The string got caught up inside once and I thought the tampon was going to be stuck there for days. I got it out really easily in the end-I had to do a few gymnastics though!

If you have a good relationship with your mum or a friend, you can ask for their help; they may be able to see the string. In the last resort, you can always go to your doctor or a clinic, but to have to do this is really very rare.

Does the string ever break?

Not that I have ever heard, though anything is possible once!

What if I forget to take out the last tampon?

It is really important not to forget to do this, but if you do, you may notice a smelly discharge from the vagina after a few days, or just a funny smell. When you do pull the tampon out, it often smells appalling.

I left a tampon in for three days once, I found out because there was this terrible smell. Ever since, I try and remember to double check.

Doctors are quite used to finding a forgotten tampon when women come into the surgery complaining of a foul smelling vaginal discharge. Don't worry if you do this once, but try to remember the next time!

I always remember a girl at school said she'd left her tampon in by accident at the end of her period - and hadn't discovered it till the next time she came on! So now I always make sure that I haven't forgotten.

Toxic shock syndrome

Some people may have heard of toxic shock syndrome, or TSS. This is a rare condition which can affect men, women and children, but about half of all cases occur in girls or women who are using tampons. Toxic shock syndrome is caused by bacteria multiplying rapidly and being absorbed into the bloodstream. This can happen if bacteria grow on the tampon, and this is one reason why it's important to change tampons regularly and not to forget to remove the last one of your period.

I heard it was bad to use tampons - didn't a girl die once or something?

Toxic shock syndrome can cause death if it is not treated quickly, but this is really very rare, so don't let it put you off using tampons.

The symptoms are:

- a temperature of over 102 ° F or 39 ° C
- shivering, trembling or fainting
- a rash
- vomiting
- diarrhoea
- a sore throat

If you have these symptoms, remove the tampon and consult your doctor immediately. Of course, even if you have these symptoms while using a tampon, you are much more likely to be going down with flu, but it is still important to check with your doctor straight away.

How do I prevent leaking?

When I haven't got enough towels or my tampon starts leaking I make my own pads out of loo paper, it's fine for a bit - as long as it isn't the shiny stuff we're given at school!

If you are desperate, loo paper is fine as a temporary measure, but it's really uncomfortable, and won't help avoid leaking in the way that a shaped towel or tampon will. You can buy these from machines in nearly all women's loos.

You can usually avoid embarrassing leaking by changing your towel or tampon regularly, although this isn't always easy.

I always think that people will know why if I go out in the middle of lessons to change my towel, but then I worry that if I wait till the end there will be a big red stain on my skirt.

As a rule, if in doubt or worrying about possible leaks, do change your towel or tampon. It's impossible to concentrate on anything else if you're worrying about whether or not any blood is going to show!

If you do leak and stain your clothing without noticing, real friends will point this out to you quietly, without making a fuss, so you can go and wash it off. If someone tries to embarrass you about it, remember that you are not the only person this has ever happened to, and tell them they should grow up!

MYTHS ABOUT PERIODS

Periods are dirty

Just because you have a period, it doesn't mean that you are dirty. In fact it shows that you have a healthy body, which is functioning properly. In some cultures women are seen as being 'unclean' when they have a period, but with increasing education this attitude is changing.

You can't have sex when you have a period

Some women feel more sexy during a period, and if neither partner minds, there is no reason not to have sex during a period. This is purely a matter of personal choice. However, some women - and men - aren't very keen on making love when the woman's period is heavy, as it can be a bit messy.

You can't get pregnant when you have a period

Actually you can - especially towards the end of your period, and if you have a short menstrual cycle. Sexually transmitted diseases, including HIV, can be passed through blood, so always use a condom.

You can't use a tampon if you are a virgin

The right time to wear a tampon is when you feel you want to. It has nothing to do with your virginity.

• QUIZ •

Question:

You're expecting your period and you need to buy some sanitary towels. When you go into the shop do you ...

a) Squirm near the shampoo for 5 minutes and creep out empty handed?

b) Put shampoo in a shopping basket (although you've got plenty at home) plus some shampoo for the dog (you don't have one), some bath-salts, soap, the kitchen sink (needless to say none of which you need) and finally a packet of sanitary towels.

c) Pick up a packet of sanitary towels.

Answers:

a) There's nothing to be embarrassed about - periods are a healthy sign and every woman gets them.

b) Carry on like this and you'll end up with no money at all! People at the check-out counter see a million and one things in baskets every day. Sanitary products are just one more item - and they won't even notice.

c) Well done, you've obviously read this chapter!

Question:

When can a girl start using tampons?

a) Only after she's had sex for the first time.
b) Only if she goes horse-riding.
c) Whenever she wants.

Answer:

a) It doesn't matter whether you have had sex or not - you can still use a tampon.
b) Vigorous exercise (including horse-riding) may cause the hymen to break or stretch, but as it doesn't completely block the entrance to the vagina anyway, you can still use a tampon whatever.
c) It's up to you when you feel you want to start using tampons. Remember though that some times it can take a while before you get used to them.

PART FOUR

Adolescence:
your changing emotions

Adolescence: your changing emotions

In the year or two before your periods start, you will have become aware of changes in your body which herald the start of puberty* or adolescence*. Along with these physical changes often comes an acute awareness of your body, and perhaps worries about how other people view you and whether or not you will be attractive to others.

Everyone reacts to these changes in different ways. Some girls may be delighted at their growing breasts, and rush out at the earliest opportunity to buy a bra. Others may be horrified, feeling that their body is growing up too fast for them. It's not at all uncommon to swing between these two extremes, one day feeling it's great to be grown up and looking forward to the new freedoms and responsibilities, and the next day wishing you could still be a child - and often behaving like one too.

Your first period is a milestone, a sign that your body and mind are really changing and you're growing up. But you're not going to change overnight from a little girl into a fully-fledged woman - the change is much more subtle than that. It is normal to feel a variety of conflicting emotions. When you get your first period people will often say things like, "So you're a real woman now." Some girls like this. Others find it really embarassing. I remember thinking, "I don't want to be a woman. Anyway, I'm not a woman, I'm only twelve!"

> When I first got my period we had a male teacher for P.E. I had to tell him why I couldn't swim (I was wearing pads) and he said 'Congratulations' and made me feel proud to have started.

Who should I talk to?

If you are having any worries about periods or the other changes that are happening to your body, it helps if there is someone to talk to. Best of all is probably your mum or dad.

> I find it easiest to chat to my mum when we're out shopping, just the two of us together.

> My mum and her friends have 'girls' nights'. They talk about everything then, and they ask me what I think and feel too.

However, not all teenage girls have good relationships with their mothers, and others may not live with their mother at all. If you are living with your father and a step-mother, it may not be obvious who to talk to.

> Dad always pretends he's got to go and mend a light-bulb or fiddle with the car if we start talking about bodies or the facts of life. Maybe it's because his mum died and he was brought up by his father and he's just not used to talking about those sort of things.

Sometimes a sympathetic older person - a grand-parent, an aunt, a friend of the family or a friend's parent, can be best.

Me and my best mate sat around with her mum one evening and she answered all our questions. I get on with my mum, but it was easier talking to Kate's mum. I don't know why really, it just wasn't so embarrassing.

An older sister will have recently been through many of the changes you are now experiencing, or you may have a good friend at school who has started her periods before you.

I wish I had an older sister to talk to about periods and stuff. I feel isolated as there are no women in my family.

If you have a good relationship with a teacher at school they can also be a source of help.

PROBLEMS WITH PARENTS

One of the main problems of adolescence is the changing relationship between you and your parents. Remember, that if adolescence is sometimes a bewildering time for you, it's equally baffling for other members of your family. They have to deal with your unpredictable moods, secrecy and sometimes odd behaviour, and the fact that one day you'll seem to be confident and outgoing and the next tearful and unsure.

I have more rows with my mum now. Sometimes I wish she'd treat me like my little sister and do things for me, and other times I just wish she'd leave me alone. That's the thing about starting your periods – once that happens you feel you're not a child any longer, but I'd like to wait a bit more before I have to grow up.

Up until now you've probably been dependent on your parents emotionally, physically and financially. Part of being a teenager usually means that this is no longer the case, although staying at school till at least 16 means that few teenagers earn their own money and contribute to the family finances. This dependence on your parents for money can often be the source of arguments.

We have big arguments about the phone. My mates are kids from school and we all ring each other up, sometimes just to chat about nothing or stuff like what we're going to wear the next day. As he's the one who pays the bill, Dad goes mad if he knows I've been on the phone for long – he keeps threatening to have it cut off.

I live with my dad and we always had problems about pocket money. He didn't give me a set amount each week and I never knew how much I was going to get. When my periods started I didn't really want to have to ask him to go off and buy me sanitary towels every month, so when I talked to him about needing pads, I also talked to him about getting a bit more money and a set sum every week and he agreed – so it all turned out really well for me in the end.

Why won't my parents let me be more independent?

You will now be choosing your own friends, developing your own hobbies and interests, and forming your own opinions - and your parents may not always approve of the new you. They may dislike your friends, think your hobbies are dangerous, and have different political opinions. However, do remember that just as you have a right to your views, so do they, especially when you are still living under their roof.

How your parents react to your adolescence will have a lot to do with their childhood and adolescence and how their parents treated them. Don't be too hard on them.

 When my daughter turned 12 she suddenly stopped confiding anything in me. Jenny used to go and have long talks with my sister about boyfriends and problems at school, but she never used to whisper a word about anything that was worrying her to me. I'd expected lots of things about the teenage years, but what I had never imagined was the sudden emotional withdrawal. It was very painful.

It is normal to want to keep some things secret from parents. Just as children don't want to know the intimate details of their parents' love life, so parents find it hard to imagine their children becoming interested in the opposite sex. This can create a barrier between parents and their children at this stage in life.

Sometimes fathers find it hard when their little girl, who used to come and sit on their knee, suddenly becomes self-conscious, and they see her growing into a young woman who will be attractive to other men. It's normal for a loving father to feel protective about his daughter and have some jealous feelings towards her boyfriends.

My father was really upset when I started my period as he felt I was no longer a child and could go off and get pregnant.

Another big issue is that of control. If you live in the same house, you need to work out rules and ways of living that are going to be acceptable to both parties. But because parents have earned the money that has paid for the house and everything in it, they usually see it as 'theirs' and feel that they have rights over what happens in it. So when you want to ask friends round or have a party, they may resist, afraid that things are going to get damaged and that they will become strangers in their own home.

Why won't they let me wear what I want?

Every adolescent usually finds a way of declaring their individuality, through the clothes they wear, their hairstyles, the music they listen to, and so on. They may like to dress outrageously to shock their parents. (Often the same children would be outraged if Mum or Dad turned up at school looking in any way odd or peculiar). Often young people try to create arguments with parents, perhaps as a way of drawing the boundaries, or finding out what is allowed and what isn't.

My mum and I have big rows about clothes. OK, she has to pay for my clothes, but what I want to wear is trainers and leggings and clothes like that - basically the clothes that she hates. She says I look like a scruff, but loads of us dress like that, not in the girlie frilly things that she used to put me in.

Why won't they let me stay out late when all my friends do?

Staying out late at night is often an issue between parents and their teenage children. Although it's easy to understand that you may be having a fantastic evening and have forgotten the time, it is natural that your parents will worry about your safety. Although unfair, this is more often the case if you are a girl. If you make sure you are back when you say you will be, your parents will learn to trust you and needn't worry unnecessarily.

When I said I'd be back at twelve, I was back at twelve, when I said I'd be back at one, I was back at one and so on. Then one night I said I was going to be really late, and they said, what time, and I said at four, and they thought for a moment and then said okay. We never used to argue about it.

How can I get them to understand my point-of-view without an argument?

In any relationship, and especially in a family where there are three, four, five or more different people to consider, you need to compromise and negotiate – in other words, to bargain. "If you let me go to so-and-so's party I'll do all my homework by Friday," or "If you let me buy that outfit I'll do all the washing up for a month..." and so on.

But compromising also means that you have to consider that the other person has a point of view as well and listen to it. Instead of the shouting matches that go on in many families, it can help to have a proper session where each person states their view at length, and the other person is not allowed to interrupt. Then the other person has their turn. Then you both think about it before you come to a decision. If you can show your parents that you can act responsibly and behave in a mature way, you will earn their respect and trust.

In any family people have very strong feelings about one another and about their lives, and it doesn't hurt to show it. We can't all be sweet and reasonable all the time. Expressing anger, love, your fears and hopes, what you hate about people and what you love about them, is much healthier than bottling them up.

It's better not to blurt out your feelings in the middle of an argument when they'll do the most damage. Both adults and teenagers can say things in the heat of the moment that they don't mean and regret later.

My parents are unhappy and I feel I can't talk to them.

Not everyone has a happy family and loving parents. Some children may have parents who are in the middle of a divorce, whose fathers or mothers are out of work and depressed, parents with serious financial problems which seem to take up all their time and energy, or even parents who are violent or abusive. In these families it's very important to find some outside source of help and support.

> I was living with my dad after my parents split up. My dad was the first person I told when I got my period and he went and got me the sanitary towels. When he told my mum she was really upset that I didn't go to her first.

Some parents may have grown up in a different culture, and may find it difficult now their children are growing up with a completely different set of rules in a new culture. The 'generation gap' conflicts can be really difficult to handle in such families.

> My parents are Hindi and are really strict. Part of the problem is that they don't understand that because most of my friends' parents aren't like that, and I live here now, I'm not like my parents who were born and brought up in India.

What do my friends think?

Most teenagers worry far too much about what other people think of them. The peer group - that is, your friends and other people your age, in your school, in your street - is very important. Young people tend to want to wear similar clothes to those of people around them, to share the same music, to do the same things. The problem is that not everyone is the same, and the clothes or hairstyle which suit one person may look awful on another. Finding your own style means experimenting a bit, and yes, sometimes you'll probably look rather strange. It happens to everyone, don't worry about it!

BOYS AND PERIODS

Boys are not creatures from another planet, although it sometimes seems that they are. If you have brothers, you'll know more about boys than if you only see them at school, but if you have no brothers and go to an all-girls school you may know very little about boys at all.

Boys and girls *are* different - there's no doubt about that. But we are all human beings, and have far more in common than you might think. Boys worry just as much as girls about what people will think of them. They also have conflicts with their parents, and, while they don't have periods, they have to cope with sometimes alarming physical changes too - their bodies shoot up, their voices break, they start to sprout body hair, have sexual feelings, and so on.

Some boys get all shy when their voices start breaking. It's the ones who are quite confident anyway who don't seem to mind. I think it's the same for girls with their periods. I'd feel quite silly if one day my voice sounded like a squeaky frog - at least periods don't make a sound.

What should I tell boys about periods?

Many boys aren't given much information about periods - as they won't have periods themselves, people often think they don't need to know about them. As a result boys often hear whispered stories and half-truths which are confusing.

Boys, too, need to be told about periods. One to one, girls often say that boys are very nice and sympathetic about periods. It's when the boys are in a gang that they may make horrible jokes or tease girls, partly because they're embarrassed and don't know what to say, partly to show off to their friends. Girls can be just as bad when they gang up together and try to make boys feel small. If you get teased about your periods, try not to get embarrassed - either ignore the culprits completely or tell them to grow up!

My sisters and mum get very snooty when they're talking about periods and things, especially my sisters. They act all grown up and treat me as if I'm just a silly little boy.

Because boys often don't know much about periods, they often want to ask you questions in order to find out - they're not just asking to be horrid or embarrass you. The kinds of questions they ask are things like "Does it hurt?" or "How much blood is there?" Just telling them the simple truth is probably the best policy, but if you don't want to, it's quite okay to say that you don't feel like answering questions right now, or answer in a general way, saying "Some girls find...".

● QUIZ ●

Question:

You have a row with your mum. Do you:

a) Go to your room, slamming the door so hard that the pictures jump off their hooks?
b) Take 10 deep breaths, apologise and try and talk things over calmly?
c) Sob into your pillow believing that she's just picking on you?

Answer:

a) For parents this can be a tricky time too - you're changing so quickly that they need time to adjust. Remember that they're basically on your side, and disagreements will generally arise because they want to protect you or want the best for you.
b) If you want to sort things out, pick the right moment to negotiate and discuss it. During the morning rush or in the middle of a row won't be such a good time! Be prepared to compromise too.
c) Sometimes it can seem as if the world and his dog is out to get at you. Becoming a teenager means that you're changing from a child to an adult - and some days it can feel as if you have a foot in both camps!

Question:

A group of the boys in your class find a packet of tampons in your bag and start giggling. Do you:

a) Go beetroot and disappear as fast as you can?

b) Ask a teacher for their support and confront the boys. What were they doing going though your bag in the first place?

Answer:

a) Try not to be embarrassed - periods are perfectly natural. If boys start teasing I'll bet they only do it when they're in a group. Tell them to grow up!

b) You could remind them that not only are they being very childish, but their mums have periods too - if they didn't, those silly lads wouldn't be there!

PART FIVE

Adolescence:
your changing body

At the start of puberty, you often start to grow very suddenly, both in height and weight. Your face becomes fuller, and your voice a little lower. Your breasts start to develop and pubic and underarm hair starts to grow.

I hated it when my body started changing, the first summer when I couldn't go swimming in just my knickers and things like that.

BREAST CHANGES

The first thing you'll notice is that your nipples and the area around them tends to darken and the nipples may stand out more. Sometimes one breast starts to grow faster than the other, but don't worry, this is normal and you won't be permanently lop-sided! Your body is not perfectly symmetrical, so you may have one breast slightly larger than the other, just like one foot may be wider than the other. Your breasts grow gradually, so it's difficult to notice the process happening, and there won't be an exact moment when you realise you have breasts. People's breasts are different sizes and though your mother's breast size may be some indication, there's no way of knowing how big your breasts will be. No breasts are 'too big' or 'too small' - there is simply a very wide variation.

I nagged my mum for ages to get me a bra. She said that they didn't sell bras to cover mosquito bites and it was my Dad who went out and got me one. I suppose I was a bit small!

Remember too that fashions change. In the 18th century painters portrayed curvy, big-breasted women, while in the 1920s the fashion was to be flat-chested. Some women even bandaged their breasts flat in order to be trendy. Today fashion still has a strong effect on how girls view their body shapes - one minute breast implants are in, the next boyish flat chested figures are admired! Try to be happy with your own shape - after all, fashions change from one month to the next!

Some girls are especially self-conscious about their breasts if they are quite flat-chested, or if their breasts are very large. Some women even consider plastic surgery to change the size and shape of their breasts. This has lots of disadvantages. Breast implants are now known to have some health risks, and breast reduction operations can cause scarring. They may also affect your ability to breastfeed a baby later on, should you want to.

You should never have these operations for purely cosmetic reasons. Give your breasts time to finish growing and learn to be happy with your shape. However, if there is a medical reason why you may need this sort of operation, make sure you always talk it over very carefully with your doctor and family or friends first.

Why are women so sensitive about the appearance of their breasts?

Women often see their breasts as the main symbol of their femininity, sexuality, and attractiveness. This is probably because their other sexual parts are hidden and are not on display to men, while the breasts are clearly visible. In fact, some researchers think that breasts developed as they did as a sexual signal to men - so it's not surprising that we use them in this way.

Of course, the main biological function of the breasts is to feed a baby, and the breasts are therefore largely made up of milk-producing glands and fatty deposits.

They are also very sensitive to the touch, so that stroking the breasts is often part of a sexual relationship. Many women also find it pleasurable to breastfeed their babies.

BODY HAIR

With adolescence, hair starts to grow in the pubic area. This is usually soft at first, but becomes more wiry and curly later on. It is often, but not always, the same colour as the hair on your head. Hair also grows under the arms, and you may notice the fine hairs on your arms and legs becoming darker and more noticeable.

When you start getting big and hairy that's when your period starts!

Removing body hair is largely a matter of fashion and culture. Some people have more body hair than others, and dark hair is more obvious than fair. Some women are happy to be hairy, feeling it is more natural, as in some Mediterranean countries such as Italy and Spain. Some women dislike this hairiness, and shave their legs and under their arms. The only problem with this is that shaving makes the hair seem thicker and it tends to be bristly as it regrows, so once you've started it's hard to stop. You can also use depilatory* creams although these tend to smell unpleasant and have the same disadvantage. Waxing is another, more expensive (and more painful!) method of removing body hair, but the regrowth is slower.

it's your choice!

SKIN CHANGES

Many girls notice that their skin changes when they reach adolescence. It may become greasier and it's very common for teenagers to develop spots. It's better to let spots come to a head and dry out naturally rather than squeezing them, as they can get infected and become even worse or leave a scar. You can always cover them up temporarily with make-up if you're going out. Chemists sell creams and lotions which may help them heal more quickly.

Some people are plagued with really bad spots, and this is called acne. If this happens to you, go and see your doctor, who can offer advice on how to treat it.

SMELL

When you reach puberty the sweat glands in your body, particularly under your arms, start to produce a stickier, smellier kind of sweat. It's important to wash under your arms and keep the area clean, otherwise you can develop an unpleasant smell - this is known as body odour or B.O.

Some girls like to use deodorant all the time, just in case, others only when they are going out to a party or playing sports. As long as you wash regularly, your natural body smell should not be unpleasant, and often people find the individual scent of their boyfriend or girlfriend attractive and sexy. The body produces substances called pheromones* in sweat which are designed to attract a mate - these substances, like musk oil, are often used as ingredients in expensive perfumes, so you may not want to completely eradicate all your natural perfume!

Vaginal deodorants can actually be harmful, as they tend to kill off the natural healthy bacteria on the skin which keep away the harmful ones. Using them can lead to vaginal infections, so it's best to avoid them. Washing between your legs regularly with good old soap and water is quite enough to keep you clean and sweet-smelling!

WEIGHT

It's normal as you grow up to put on weight. Girls in particular put on fat at puberty, and their body changes into a more curvaceous womanly shape by putting on fat in certain areas. If you eat healthily and take exercise, you're unlikely to become overweight.

Trying to stop these changes

It's impossible to prevent yourself from growing up. Your body will change whatever you try and do to stop it - it has its own timetable. Sometimes girls have such a strong fear of growing up that they try to stop the process by starving themselves. This is called anorexia. This illness can prevent the development of adult curves including breasts, and can even stop a girl having periods. However, there is a terrible cost to all this, and anyone who finds that they are obsessed with their weight, deliberately avoiding food, or bingeing and then making themselves sick (known as bulimia), needs to talk either to their parents or another adult they can trust, or seek help from a doctor immediately. These are serious illnesses which can be life-threatening, so do get help if you feel this might be a problem for you.

DEVELOPING SEXUALLY

Women's sex organs, unlike men's, are hidden either inside the body or between the folds of skin between your legs. The diagram below shows what you will see if you part the outer lips (labia majora) and look at yourself - this is much easier with a mirror! You will see two ridges of skin, the inner lips or labia minora, inside which are the vaginal entrance and the clitoris. The entrance to the vagina is not easily visible, but you should be able to see the clitoris under a small hood of skin. It looks a bit like a small round button, and is very sensitive to touch.

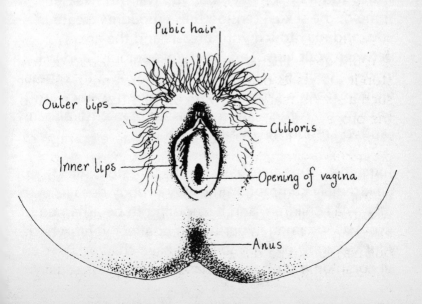

When a woman is sexually excited, the lips, known as the labia, swell and become darker in colour, as the blood flow increases in this area. The inner lips and clitoris swell too, and become even more sensitive to touch. The walls of the vagina lubricate, producing a discharge which some girls may notice on their pants.

It's normal for the vagina to produce some discharge all the time, and this discharge changes throughout a woman's cycle. Only if the discharge is very thick, yellow, irritating or smelly do you need to check with a doctor, in case you have an infection.

Sexual feelings

A t some point you will probably become aware of sexual feelings for the first time. This is usually centred around fancying someone or fantasising about them. You may well feel that you want to release some of the sexual tension these thoughts create in you, and may touch your breasts and the area between your legs. This is very pleasurable, and will increase your sexual feelings. You may find that these feelings reach a climax and you may experience an orgasm, or 'come' - this is a feeling of intense pleasure centred around the genital region.

Touching yourself sexually is called masturbation*, and is extremely common. Almost everybody does it, even very small children, and it's nothing to be ashamed of. (Nor will it damage your health or affect your periods, your eyesight, or your ability to have children later on; all common myths about masturbation.) It is usually a very private activity (although occasionally girls and boys will masturbate together within a sexual relationship). It's a way of finding out about your sexual feelings and appreciating and understanding your own body.

GETTING TO KNOW BOYS

At some stage in your teenage years you'll probably start 'going out' with boys. There is, of course, a difference between having friends who happen to be boys, and in going out with a boy on a date. There may be some boys at school, or friends of your brothers, or neighbours, who you get on with, play games with when they're around, walk home from school with or play with over the garden wall. You may play music with a boy in the school orchestra or act opposite him in the school play, or you might help one another with your homework.

At a certain point you may feel that you want to get to know this boy better. You may find you're really fancying him – thinking he's the brightest, best-looking or the nicest boy in the class and fantasising about being on your own with him, or even imagining situations in which you might rescue him from danger. Often these relationships are just a crush. He may not be interested in you, and you might find that if he did ask you out, you wouldn't have a clue what to say to him and would feel awkward and embarrassed. Crushes are not silly; almost everybody has them. They are a safe way of trying out the emotions of love and attraction and playing them out in a way in which no-one's feelings get seriously hurt.

Very often girls develop a crush first on a pop star, a film star or some completely unattainable man so that they can test out their feelings without even having to meet the person concerned. Sometimes you may have a crush on a much older boy, such as a sixth-former or a friend's older brother who's at college, someone who would never be interested in you. Sometimes a crush can develop into a more serious relationship if you do go out with the boy concerned. But usually it doesn't. It may be quite another boy who you eventually become friends with and go out with.

It's quite common for a girl to develop her first crush on another girl, especially if she's at a single sex school and doesn't see many boys. Often it's a teacher or an older girl such as a sixth former. This doesn't necessarily mean that you're a lesbian and will only ever fall in love with girls. If you do find later that you are attracted to someone of the same sex, some people, especially older people, may be prejudiced against you, but as long as you are both happy together, there is nothing wrong or abnormal about being in love with someone of the same sex.

Despite the growing sexual equality between men and women, it's still true that, on the whole, a boy asks a girl if she'll go out with him and then the girl decides. Girls who ask boys out may sometimes be unfairly thought of as 'easy'. But in fact most boys would really appreciate someone else doing the asking, as they have to face the possibility of rejection every time they ask a girl out. So, why not go ahead and ask out whoever you want - you never know, they might say yes!

Getting physical

If you do go out with a boy, at some point the question of whether or not to kiss him will come up. The most important thing is to do what you feel comfortable with. You may feel happy to hold hands, sit close to one another, and to kiss one another on the cheek to say hello or goodbye. At some stage you may want to kiss your boyfriend on the mouth. 'French' kissing is when you open your mouth and either the boy or the girl puts their tongue inside the other's mouth. There are no rules about this; you do it if you want to, and if it makes you uncomfortable, then don't. A sensitive person will respond to your signals and won't force himself on you if you're not enjoying it.

Having sex or making love

At some point as you grow up, when you have a close relationship with a boy, you will start thinking about whether you want to have sex. This is a big step to take, and it can be difficult to make a decision. This may be because you are not sure of the boy's feelings, but also you may not be sure about your own.

Many of us are still brought up with the romantic idea that there is one perfect partner for each of us, and that we should wait until he comes along before jumping into bed. In fact it's not that simple, and today it's much more common for people to have more than one sexual relationship before they finally commit themselves to one person.

But before you consider a sexual relationship, you want to make sure that you are really valued, that you have a good relationship with the boy and feel deeply about one another, and know that he will not let you down. If you have sex with a boy only to discover that he doesn't care about you and was just using you, you are going to feel very hurt and betrayed. It will be the same for him if you have sex with him without really caring about him as a person.

Sexuality is a very powerful force, and, while you may think that you are grown up enough to handle it, even much older, experienced people find that they can be overwhelmed by the strong emotions which are involved. Even if you have a strong and committed relationship with your boyfriend, having sex will put new pressures on you both - such as dealing with contraception, and being prepared for a possible pregnancy.

This is one reason why adults, especially parents, often want to protect young people from sexual experiences which can be emotionally painful. If you are in doubt about whether to have sex with your boyfriend, remember that hardly anyone has ever regretted waiting, while many do regret having a sexual relationship too early.

Legally you are considered too young to have sex until you reach the age of 16. However, some young people do have sex before this age, and it's important that they talk to an understanding adult about contraception and any problems which may result from a sexual relationship, before starting to have sex. Doctors, Brook Advisory Centres (see page 96) and other young people's clinics will see young people in confidence, without informing parents or others unless you want them to, although they may point out the advantages of sharing your concerns with your family.

If you do reach the stage when you and your boyfriend feel ready to have sex, you should always insist he wears a condom to protect both of you against sexually transmitted diseases, including the AIDS virus, HIV. If he won't wear a condom, dump him. Your life is more important than his feelings about wearing a condom and if he doesn't see this too, he isn't the right one for you.

There are many different types of contraception available, and these can be obtained free of charge from a family planning clinic, Brook Advisory Centre or doctor. Some types of contraception, such as the pill, may affect periods, as they involve taking artificial hormones, but most doctors will explain this before prescribing contraception. Any consultation with a doctor or clinic will be confidential, whatever your age.

Menstrual Calendar

Circle the dates you start your period each month and work out the number of days between them. This is your menstrual cycle. Count the same number of days again from the beginning of your last period and you should be able to get an idea of when you are likely to come on. See how close your prediction is to the day you actually do start!

January

1	2	3	4	5	6	7
8	9	10	11	12	13	14
15	16	17	18	19	20	21
22	23	24	25	26	27	28
29	30	31				

February

1	2	3	4	5	6	7
8	9	10	11	12	13	14
15	16	17	18	19	20	21
22	23	24	25	26	27	28
(29)						

March

1	2	3	4	5	6	7
8	9	10	11	12	13	14
15	16	17	18	19	20	21
22	23	24	25	26	27	28
29	30	31				

April

1	2	3	4	5	6	7
8	9	10	11	12	13	14
15	16	17	18	19	20	21
22	23	24	25	26	27	28
29	30					

May

1	2	3	4	5	6	7
8	9	10	11	12	13	14
15	16	17	18	19	20	21
22	23	24	25	26	27	28
29	30	31				

June

1	2	3	4	5	6	7
8	9	10	11	12	13	14
15	16	17	18	19	20	21
22	23	24	25	26	27	28
29	30					

July

1	2	3	4	5	6	7
8	9	10	11	12	13	14
15	16	17	18	19	20	21
22	23	24	25	26	27	28
29	30	31				

August

1	2	3	4	5	6	7
8	9	10	11	12	13	14
15	16	17	18	19	20	21
22	23	24	25	26	27	28
29	30	31				

September

1	2	3	4	5	6	7
8	9	10	11	12	13	14
15	16	17	18	19	20	21
22	23	24	25	26	27	28
29	30					

October

1	2	3	4	5	6	7
8	9	10	11	12	13	14
15	16	17	18	19	20	21
22	23	24	25	26	27	28
29	30	31				

November

1	2	3	4	5	6	7
8	9	10	11	12	13	14
15	16	17	18	19	20	21
22	23	24	25	26	27	28
29	30					

December

1	2	3	4	5	6	7
8	9	10	11	12	13	14
15	16	17	18	19	20	21
22	23	24	25	26	27	28
29	30	31				

Glossary

Adolescence. The state of passing from childhood to maturity. See **Puberty**.

Amenorrhoea. Sometimes, particularly when we become over-stressed or worried, or aren't eating properly, our periods may stop altogether. This is known as amenorrhoea.

Anus. The exit of the alimentary canal or food passage, which is next to the vagina. Food passes down the alimentary canal from the mouth and is either digested and used by the body, or got rid of as waste-matter, through the anus, in the form of faeces.

Cervix. The entrance to the uterus or womb at the top of the vagina.

Clitoris. The clitoris lies at the top of the vulva where the inner lips meet. It can feel like a tiny pea. Though small, it is full of nerve endings which make it feel sensitive and good to touch.

Depilatory cream. A cream which is used to remove hair from various parts of the body. Depilation is the process of removing hair.

Diuretics. Pills which help lessen water retention, and encourage emptying of the bladder.

Discharge. This is a fluid from the vagina which you will see on your pants. This is normally clear and colourless but varies during the month (whiter during ovulation, browner just before a period, for example). If the discharge is very thick, yellow, irritating or smelly you need to get it checked out by a doctor, as you may have an infection.

Dysmenorrhoea. The pain that may accompany your period.

Ejaculation. This is when semen (the fluid containing sperm) squirts out of a man's penis as he orgasms or 'comes'.

Fallopian Tubes. The two Fallopian tubes are each about three inches long and are on either side of the uterus. They are the paths through which the egg travels on its journey down from the ovary to the uterus.

Hormones. The changes that take place in our bodies during puberty are caused by hormones. These are chemicals that our body produces. The ovaries produce the hormones oestrogen and progesterone.

Hymen. This is a thin layer of skin that covers part of the entrance to the vagina. Some girls are born without a hymen, and others may stretch or break it naturally through exercise, or later, the first time they have sexual intercourse. However, except very rarely, the hymen never completely seals the vagina so the blood from a period can always come through.

Labia. The two lips of skin (*labia* is the Latin word for lips) that cover the inner parts of the vulva, the entrance to the vagina, the clitoris and the urethra.

Masturbation. This is when a boy or girl touches themselves sexually in the genital region to create a feeling of pleasure.

Menopause. This is the time in a woman's life when she stops having periods and around two years later ceases to be able to get pregnant.

Menstruation. This is the most common name for a period. Some people find it hard to talk openly about periods, so they call periods by lots of other names, such as: 'the curse', 'on the rag', 'blobbing', 'time of the month', being 'on', 'Arsenal's playing at home', 'feeling poorly', 'monthlies' or 'got a visitor'.

Menstrual cycle. The words menstruation and menstrual come from the latin word *menses*, meaning month. Regular monthly bleeding is called a menstrual cycle.

Metabolism. This is the sum of all the chemical changes that take place within the body. An example of one of these chemical changes is the conversion of sugar into energy.

Oestrogen. A female hormone which is responsible for the physical changes you will see taking place in your body during puberty, such as breast development.

Ovary. The ovaries are either side of the uterus. They are about the size of a thumbnail and contain thousands of tiny egg cells. When a girl is born her ovaries will already contain 1-2 million egg cells. These egg cells will gradually lessen throughout childhood and by the time a girl reaches puberty there will be about 300,000 egg cells left. A girl will release 400 - 500 egg cells during her lifetime.

Ovulation. This is what happens when the ovaries start to release an egg. Girls usually start their periods after their ovaries have begun to release egg cells.

Ovum. This comes from the Latin word, *ovum*, meaning egg. An ovum is a single egg cell.

Pheromones.These are chemical substances, secreted from the body, which influence the behaviour of other people, for example, the substances in sweat are designed to attract a mate.

Pituitary. A gland at the base of the brain which controls the hormones in the body.

Placenta. The placenta is the structure which links the unborn child to its mother within the womb. The placenta passes food and blood to the baby and transports waste matter away from it.

Pre-menstrual syndrome/tension. PMS or PMT normally happens in the two weeks before a period starts - generally between ovulation and bleeding. PMS covers a range of emotional and physical symptoms. These can include mood swings, when you become more irritable or touchy than usual and find it hard to concentrate. You may also notice that your weight changes, and you may feel fat and bloated. Many girls also experience food cravings, especially for sweet or salty food. It's important to bear in mind that PMS can be worse if you are tired or stressed or your diet isn't good.

Progesterone. One of the female hormones responsible for the physical changes during puberty.

Puberty. This word comes from the Latin *puber*, meaning grown-up. Puberty is the word used to describe the time when girl's and boy's bodies start to change from those of children to those of adults.

Sanitary Protection. This includes all the different towels, pads and tampons you can buy to absorb the blood during a period. There are many different makes, shapes, sizes - and prices! Most will say on the packet whether they are suitable for the first few days of a period, when bleeding is heaviest, or the end, when the bleeding is less. Shopping around and asking friends may help you decide which brand to try.

Urethra. An opening just below the clitoris connected to the bladder. Urine comes out of the urethra.

Uterus. Another word for the womb. When a woman is pregnant this is the place where the developing baby grows inside her for nine months. The uterus is an organ made up of strong stretchy muscles, so it can grow with the unborn baby. It looks rather like an upside down pear and is about the same size. It is attached to the vagina at the base (where the pear's stalk would be) and the two Fallopian tubes are on either side at the top.

Vagina. The tube that leads from the vulva on the outside of a girl's body to the uterus. It's normally about three and a half inches long, and the walls lie flat against each other. But it's stretchy and can fit a tampon and even a baby, as this is the passage down which a baby travels when it's born.

Vulva. The outer sex organs between a girl's legs; including the clitoris and the opening to the vagina, the urethra and the labia.

Useful addresses

Brook Advisory Centre
165 Grays Inn Road
London WC1X 8UD   Tel: 0171 713 9000
24-hour recorded information helpline: 0171 617 8000

Brook runs local centres throughout the country offering
confidential contraceptive advice and counselling for young
people. All teenagers and young people are welcome.

Family Planning Association
27-35 Mortimer Street
London W1N 7RJ   Tel: 0171 636 7866

Healthwise, the Family Planning Association's bookshop, runs a
mail-order service, and the FPA can give information on all
aspects of sexuality and birth control and the address of your
nearest family planning clinic.

Health Education Authority
Hamilton House
Mabledon Place
London WC1H 9TX   Tel: 0171 383 3833

The Health Education Authority (HEA) publish leaflets and books
on a range of health topics, which are usually available at a local
health promotion clinic (check in the phone book for your
nearest clinic).

Youth Access
Magazine Business Centre
11 Newarke Street
Leicester LE1 5SS

Youth Access can give information on local young people's
counselling and advice centres in England, Scotland and Wales.

Childline   Tel: 0800 1111

This is a free confidential telephone helpline for any young
person in trouble or danger.